PMP Journey: From Resistance to Above Target

A Mindset-Driven System for PMP Candidates Who Are Done Guessing

By Cartraill Love, MBA, PMP

Matters of Matters Publishing

2026

Disclaimer

This book is a personal memoir and study methodology guide based on my own PMP® journey, exam preparation, and lessons learned through failure, correction, and eventual success. It reflects my personal interpretations, frameworks, and strategies developed while preparing for and passing the PMP® exam.

PMP®, PMI®, PMBOK®, and PMI Study Hall® are registered trademarks or service marks of the Project Management Institute, Inc. Their use in this book is for identification and reference purposes only. I am not affiliated with, endorsed by, or sponsored by PMI®. This book is an independent work and does not represent the official positions of PMI®.

Any references to third-party resources, including Rita Mulcahy's PMP® Exam Prep, Prepsaret, David McLachlan, PMBOK® guides, or the Agile Practice Guide, are included for commentary, study reference, and educational discussion only. No third-party content has been reproduced as official source material. The scenarios, worked examples, and frameworks in this book are original to this work unless otherwise noted.

This book is intended for educational and informational purposes only. It is not a substitute for the official PMP® Examination Content Outline, current PMI® publications, or your own professional judgment. Because exam content, domain weightings, and supporting standards may change over time, readers should always confirm the most current PMP® exam requirements and PMI® guidance before finalizing a study plan.

No guarantee of exam results is made or implied. Your outcome will depend on your own preparation, application, timing, and judgment.

Release Note for 2026 Readers

This edition reflects the PMP exam structure in effect during my own exam attempts and the lessons I learned while preparing for that version of the test. As of this writing, PMI has announced a revised PMP exam planned to take effect on July 9, 2026, with rebalanced domain weights and additional emphasis on AI, sustainability, stakeholder engagement, and value delivery. Candidates should always confirm the current effective date and details on pmi.org.

The July 9, 2026 exam also shifts the predictive versus agile balance. Under the exam structure I prepared for, PMI described the content as being approximately half predictive and half agile/hybrid. In the July 2026 update, PMI describes the balance as roughly 40% predictive and 60% adaptive/agile and hybrid across all three domains. This signals that PMI expects candidates to be comfortable with adaptive thinking in every part of the exam, not just in process questions.

If you are testing on or after July 9, 2026, use the latest PMI Examination Content Outline alongside this book, and treat PMBOK 8 as a principles and value-delivery companion — especially for AI, sustainability, stakeholder engagement, and benefits realization — rather than as a memorization list.

The systems in this book — the Book of Wrongs, the 5 PM Instincts, and the PM Response Order — apply to the new exam exactly as they apply to the current one. PMI is not changing what it rewards; it is expanding the contexts in which it tests it. Appendix D (PMBOK 8 Cheat Sheet) maps the new vocabulary to the instincts you are already building.

Table of Contents

INTRODUCTION

This book is dedicated to those committed not only to obtaining their Project Management Professional (PMP) certification, but also to those who refuse to give up on themselves while balancing life and overcoming adversity along the way.

It is about trusting the process and maintaining a growth mindset. Even while watching others move into positions of recognition and opportunity — some with less formal education, fewer certifications, and different levels of corporate experience — I stayed committed to my own growth, and you should too.

Investing in myself became questionable at times because leveling up in knowledge did not always seem to materialize the benefits I expected in certain business arenas. That forced me to confront something: progress is not always tied to qualifications alone. That realization could have discouraged me. Instead, it made me think differently about how to overcome the obstacles placed before me. Every time I wanted to advance, I found it necessary to add more to my utility belt to make it harder to deny me. Here is the catch: I did not just want to grow. I wanted to be in a position to help create the changes needed for the people affected, or lead others in bringing those changes to life, even in environments where resistance existed.

Upon completing my MBA, that clarity turned into action. I thought to myself: if not the MBA, then surely the PMP would help propel me forward in the corporate arena, or as an entrepreneur who wanted to complete projects in the most efficient way. That said, the journey to obtain the PMP meant more than another credential. It was a means of refining myself once again in thinking, leading, and execution. It was not a walk in the park. Obtaining the PMP was more like a journey through the park, one that required observation, endurance, and learning from everything around me. I failed the PMP not once, but twice — on March 14, 2025, and again on March 4, 2026. Those failures weighed heavily on me. Still, I saw the areas I needed to improve, picked myself up, and went on to pass on March 17, 2026, with Above Target in all three domains: People, Process, and Business Environment.

Passing the exam was the deliverable. Who I became in the process was the true outcome.

This is not a traditional PMP exam prep book. It will not walk you line by line through every process group or every Agile ceremony. You either already have those resources, or you will gain insight into some of the resources I used throughout my journey. This book is for when you have done all that and still are not getting the results you want, or when you simply want someone's testimony of passing and what they did to earn Above Target in all three domains.

This One Is for YOU

If any of the following reflects your experience, keep reading:

- You are scoring low on mock exams and not seeing improvement.

- You have failed a mock exam or the PMP exam once — or multiple times — and you are ready to pass.

- You understand the material, yet still second-guess your first instinct and doubt yourself.

- You need guidance and a system from someone who has actually experienced the exam.

- You have studied over and over, yet you are still getting questions wrong.

Author's Note

After my PMP journey, I felt inspired and compelled to draft this book within 12 days of passing with Above Target in all three domains. The obstacles, the mistakes, and the times I felt like flinging the book across the room in frustration — just joking, but the frustration was real — were all part of the process. The time it took and the mental energy it required were real too. This book is my gift to you.

How to Use This Book

The chapters ahead tell the story of how I failed, what I learned, and what finally worked. Before you begin, here is a reference guide you can return to at any point in your journey.

If you are a first-time exam taker:

Read Chapters 1 through 5 to understand the mindset traps, the shift from your own instincts to PMI's way of thinking, and the foundations of the PM Mindset, PM Alignment, PM Instinct, and the Book of Wrongs before you begin practicing questions. Then read Chapter 6 to understand the frustration phase that often appears when your knowledge is growing but your scores are not yet moving.

As you work through your study resources, recommended options include the relevant PMBOK, Rita, Study Hall, David McLachlan on YouTube, and Prepsaret. Build your Book of Wrongs during the final 30 to 45 days before the exam, especially in the last 13 days.

If you have failed at least once:

Breathe. Everything will work out. Give yourself grace and keep going.

Start with the Introduction, then read Chapters 2 through 7. Ask yourself whether you see overlaps in our journeys. Print your Exam Analysis or keep your score report beside you as you read.

Pay close attention to Chapters 5 through 7, where the book moves from PM Mindset and PM Instinct into frustration, correction, and the 13-Day Turnaround. Then read Chapter 11 to decode your score report more precisely.

Use the guidance in Chapter 7 to create your own Book of Wrongs and design a 30- to 45-day plan, or a 13-day plan, but not a full restart.

If your exam is in 2 to 4 weeks:

Review Chapters 5 through 9 — the Three Stages of Growth, the 5 PM Instincts, the frustration phase, the 13-Day

Turnaround, the breakthrough, and methodology recognition.

Then read Chapter 11 to sharpen your targeted correction strategy.

After Chapter 7, build or refine your Book of Wrongs and use it as a daily tool. Focus on why PMI's answers are the way they are, not on adding more material.

Overview of the Stages

Stage 1 — PM Mindset (Chapters 1–5): You build the foundation. You understand what PMI rewards. You can often identify the right answer, but it still takes effort, structure, and deliberate reasoning.

Stage 2 — PM Alignment (Chapters 6–7): You do your own retrospective. You use the Book of Wrongs to turn wrong patterns into corrected thinking. Weak task areas begin to improve because your preparation becomes targeted.

Stage 3 — PM Instinct (Chapters 8–10): The PM Mindset has moved from conscious effort to natural response. PM Alignment is no longer something you force; it is something you operate from. You answer with greater confidence, clarity, and instinct.

The Five PM Instincts

- Analyze Before You Act
- Coach or Facilitate Before Escalating
- Protect Compliance and Quality
- Recognize the Methodology

- Trust Your Trained First Answer

The 13-Day Turnaround — Accelerated Path to Growth

1. Read your Exam Analysis honestly.
2. Write down your weak tasks and turn them into a checklist.
3. Go task by task in Study Hall.
4. Cross-reference with your main PMP book.
5. Take notes and track what you missed.
6. Quiz yourself and practice with a study partner.
7. Use the last 3–5 days to build your Book of Wrongs.

Final Note

This book is not meant to replace your primary study resources. It is meant to help you think differently about the exam, correct the patterns that are costing you points, and build the PM Mindset, PM Alignment, and PM Instinct needed to pass.

THE SYSTEM AT A GLANCE

How This Book Works as a Complete Operating System

STAGE 1 — PM MINDSET

You understand what PMI rewards. You can arrive at the right answer, but it takes deliberate effort.

Output: The toolkit is built.

→ Chapters 1–5

STAGE 2 — PM ALIGNMENT

You confront the specific ways your thinking diverges from the exam. You use the Book of Wrongs to convert wrong answers into correction data. The 13-Day Turnaround is the accelerated repair path for this stage.

Output: The gaps are identified and closed.

→ Chapters 6–7 + 13-Day Turnaround

STAGE 3 — PM INSTINCT

The framework fires automatically. You recognize the right answer before you finish reading the options. The 5 PM Instincts are the operating system.

Output: Above Target performance under real exam conditions.

→ Chapters 8–10

THE 5 PM INSTINCTS — Your Operating System

- #1 Analyze Before You Act
- #2 Coach or Facilitate Before Escalating
- #3 Protect Compliance and Quality
- #4 Recognize the Methodology

- #5 Trust Your Trained First Answer

THE 13-DAY TURNAROUND — Accelerated Repair Path

Score report → Task-level repair → Book of Wrongs consolidation → 50-question reps → Instinct

Use this map as a compass. Every time you feel lost in the preparation process, come back here and locate yourself. What stage are you in? What is the tool for this stage? What is the output?

CHAPTER 1

The Denial, the Failure, and the Resilience

Shortly after notifying my department that I had obtained my MBA, I began searching for ways to get my PMP sponsored. I went through the proper channels, spoke with my manager, and asked for support. I was advised to write out why I wanted the PMP and what benefit it would bring to the department. I put together a full page: a clear scope outlining the cost, the value of the certification, and how I could leverage it to help the department. I sent it off and waited.

The response came back: it didn't fit the budget. And even if it did, it would not be until the next fiscal quarter, with no guarantee.

That answer was unacceptable. I made up my mind that I was going to get my PMP, and no one was going to stop me. I began doing research, reached out to a few individuals, and had several conversations. Through those conversations, I was pointed toward a PMP bootcamp. I enrolled, notified the proper channels, and was met with pushback once again, but I prevailed. I joined the bootcamp alongside others who were just as determined to pass. There, I received Rita's PMP Exam

Prep, additional study materials, and met my first study partner.

We studied together on and off for nearly a year. We shared resources, worked through the material, created our own case studies, and ran simulations to examine why one answer was correct over the others. On the surface, our preparation looked nearly identical. But as exam day approached, one difference began to show: I focused more on applying the concepts, while my study partner focused more on understanding the structure of the questions themselves. We set our exam dates. I took mine and failed. My study partner took theirs and passed.

Looking back, I understand what happened. My study partner had tapped into the PM Mindset — the way PMI expects a project manager to think and prioritize — while I was applying the concepts through my own lens, the way I would act on a real project. Those are not the same thing, and the exam knows the difference.

My first Exam Analysis reflected what many candidates see: People and Business Environment at Target, with the Process domain either Below Target or Needs Improvement. I reviewed the results, but I did not formulate an actual plan. I treated the score report like feedback on a performance rather than a roadmap for preparing differently. That distinction cost me more time than it needed to.

Instead of letting those two forces — organizational resistance on one side, a failing score report on the other — knock me down, they became fuel. If support and timing were not guaranteed, I would rely on the drive within me and keep my foot on the pedal until I passed.

What the denial taught me: the system will not always meet you where you are, and depending upon who you are, institutional support might feel more like resistance than support. But you have to decide that your preparation will be undeniable whether anyone shows up for you or not. That is what separates the candidate who eventually passes from the one who never fully commits.

CHAPTER 2

The Noise: Everyone Has the Answers

After my first attempt, I thought to myself, let me find out what others had experienced, what helped them pass, and what resources they were using. I found groups, individuals, YouTube videos, courses, and practice exams. I found answers. I found resources. The problem was, I did not filter what would work for me and what would not. I was carrying a lot of noise in my head and a heavy utility belt full of resources I kept testing along the way. Truthfully, it had me all over the place. The effort was there, but I was lacking the proper alignment because I thought doing more with more resources meant knowing more. I was wrong. The exam showed me that. Even though I thought I was operating at the level the PMP required — applying the knowledge to actual projects, making real decisions, dealing with real stakeholders — I still was not thinking the way PMI expected me to think. In my mind, I was "doing the work," so I expected the experience to help me with decision-making. The exam showed me that the Process domain was the area where I needed the most improvement.

As I reflect, the first failure was not all about Process. It was more about the way I practiced. Doing the quizzes and mock exams mattered. I read and understood the material, but I only completed one mock exam and a couple of quizzes, and never truly dissected my wrong answers. My early preparation was geared more toward reading, applying, and remembering. It was never really geared toward what to expect on the exam or what mindset to have. At that point, I needed to step away, recharge, and recalibrate with renewed energy to try again.

This time, I developed a plan and followed it, but somewhere along the way that same noise came back, and the experimenting with different resources started all over again. I completed multiple exams this time around, but I still limited myself to more reading and less application, and that hurt just as much. The noise was louder. I moved between frameworks and tips from multiple PMP gurus on YouTube: "Always escalate," "Never escalate," "Always choose servant leadership." But the scenarios did not always match the advice.

The truth is, I lacked a system for tracking my wrong answers, deciphering what was right and wrong, identifying patterns, and developing the mindset that aligned with PMI for project managers. I was just filling notebook after notebook, hoping I would retain the information that way.

On the day of the exam, after I completed it, I felt depleted. I just wanted to rest. Something told me I had not passed. Maybe it was the fact that I rushed through the final 10–15 questions, or maybe I still did not have the right mindset. All I know is that when I checked my results the following day, they looked worse than before. I still made Target in the Business Environment and People domains, but in Process I had actually moved from Below Target to Needs Improvement. I was crushed and angry at myself.

More Questions, More Answers?

Doing the same thing in a different way led to the same result, if not worse. More notebooks, more remembering, more late nights, more application, more questions, and more mock exams were not the answer. That is where the fall can happen: when you walk right over a trap disguised as a bridge. Volume without analysis is just repeated noise you do not need.

Sometimes we need a new voice of reason or support. Doing things alone is fine, but in this case, choosing the right volume and the right study partner mattered. Honestly, that was one of my critical turning points. My new study partner delivered a message that changed everything: we needed the PM Mindset to get through these questions.

Additionally, extracting lessons from missed questions mattered. Every wrong answer is data, and the moment we decide to put it under the microscope and break it down to its foundation, we begin to see similar questions in the same light. That is what the next chapter is about: shifting from experience to framework.

CHAPTER 3

PM Levels of Attainment

The ultimate goal of this chapter is to shift our thinking from our own way to the way of the project manager. Imagine this as a discipline. When you enter the dojo, you learn the fundamentals in order to advance. Remember that.

Failing forced me to examine my entire approach. I entered the PM dojo with the wrong thinking — my way instead of the foundational, disciplined way of the PM. The structure provided, such as the information most often found in PMI Study Hall, for the People, Process, and Business Environment domains listed the tasks to know as the framework. When I slowed down and focused more on the structure, I started getting it right.

I stopped asking, What would I do? Instead, I started asking, What phase are we in? What task is this? What keywords do I see? What approach do I need to take? It was no longer about what I thought should be done. Not only was I developing the PM Mindset, I was also capturing the right data and beginning to use the right resources to build it.

Being wrong became lessons learned that I added to what would become my Book of Wrongs, which I called Kitabu Cha Makosa (Swahili for "Book of Wrongs"). I really wanted to get my makosa right going forward. In that book, I recorded what I got wrong and why PMI considered the other answer right. Part of developing and acquiring the mindset led to alignment with what the Project Management Institute (PMI) wanted, and that led to what I call the PM Instinct.

In the PMP bootcamp, it seemed that knowing less was actually knowing more. There were individuals who were already hired as project managers and knew more, yet got more questions wrong. Meanwhile, some who knew less about the actual work got more questions right. To learn more and get more questions right, you must enter the PM dojo with an empty cup, ready to be filled, rather than one that is already half full — or already full.

Hone the PM Mindset, align with PMI's way of thinking, and acquire the PM Instinct. These were the PM levels of attainment that would eventually help me pass.

CHAPTER 4

The Mindset, the Alignment, and the Instinct

Before going further, I want to be clear: PM Instinct is not official PMI terminology. It is a concept that emerged for me through the trial and error of the PMP journey. PM Instinct is my coaching term for the internal navigation system that develops once a PMP candidate gains the knowledge, builds the PM Mindset, and aligns that mindset with PMI's way of thinking, discipline, and rules of engagement.

The PM Mindset is a conscious framework. PM Instinct is that same framework firing automatically when it matters most. It is the difference between having to think through every move and responding correctly because the right thinking has already been trained into you.

PM Instinct is not automatic at first. It develops through habit, through repeated exposure, repeated correction, and repeated alignment with PMI's way of thinking until the right response begins to come naturally.

The distinction between the mindset, the alignment, and the instinct deserves its own chapter because understanding the mindset leads to alignment, and proper alignment leads to the development of instinct. That instinct begins to operate subconsciously after the information has first been accepted consciously. The PM Mindset helps us identify what PMI rewards and what PMI does not. That distinction matters if you want to pass the PMP.

The foundations of the mindset can include assessing before acting, being a servant leader, removing impediments, protecting value, identifying and involving the right stakeholders throughout the project, and selecting the most relevant project methodology (predictive, agile, or hybrid), to name a few. Those foundations within the mindset eventually allow instinct to take the wheel and guide you toward the right answer without arguing over whether it is correct. The right answer comes before doubt has a chance to argue with it.

The instinct did not come from reading more pages. Prior to my final push, I had already filled multiple notebooks, generated documents, and taken endless notes from multiple resources. More notes and more reading did not solve the full problem. The true breakthrough came when I read the exam analysis, the test reports, and quiz results thoroughly, went task by task in Study Hall, tied weak tasks to the right chapters and lessons, and only then consolidated everything into a final review system, what I would call the Book of Wrongs.

I also had to reprioritize the backlog of my life to create the capacity to study at least five times a week. Some sessions lasted longer than others. That matters, because instinct is built through frequency and recovery, not random bursts of motivation. It required vision and discipline.

Knowing when to stop mattered too. I noticed that when I went on a streak of correct answers followed by a streak of getting questions wrong that I actually knew, it was fatigue. I had to give myself grace. I realized something critical for the exam: I was building endurance for it. I started treating my study sessions the way someone trains for a major event, like a 5K run. Each session was progressive, deliberate, and long enough to train my mind to stay sharp for the full four hours.

PM Mindset	PM Instinct
Conscious use of the PMI framework and principles.	The PMI framework and principles respond automatically.
You can reason your way to the correct answer, even under pressure.	The correct answer arrives before you finish reading the options, even under pressure.
You might doubt your correct first answer and sometimes change it to the wrong one.	You select the right answer and don't second-guess yourself.
Mock exam scores are up and down; your results vary a lot.	Mini-exam scores stabilize near the top of your range.

Sign you have developed the PM Mindset: You read an exam question, identify the right answer, then doubt yourself and change it to a wrong one. You actually knew it. You just didn't trust your PMI-aligned thinking.

Sign you have the PM Instinct: You developed the PM Mindset, you quickly spot and discard the wrong options, and trust your first answer to be correct. You trust yourself.

PM Mindset Meaning

The PM Mindset is the conscious and consistent application of PMI-aligned thinking. When you have developed the PM Mindset, you can analyze a scenario and reason your way to the correct answer, even if it still takes effort. You understand the principles, frameworks, and processes, and you can apply them correctly.

At this level, you can usually explain why an answer is right. Even when you choose the wrong option, you often realize afterward that you originally understood the better choice. That is the difference between knowledge and trust.

Mindset is your toolkit. It means you know the material well enough to explain it, teach it, and use it deliberately. But under the pressure of a four-hour exam with 180 questions, fatigue, ambiguity, and time pressure can all interfere with execution. You may know the right answer and still fail to select it.

That is why the PM Mindset is necessary, but not sufficient on its own. It is the foundation, not the finish line.

Many study methods help candidates build the mindset but stop there. That is where many candidates plateau. The breakthrough happens when the PM Mindset is trained deeply enough to become PM Instinct: the ability to recognize the right answer faster, dismiss weak choices with confidence, and trust the PMI-aligned response without second-guessing yourself.

PM Instinct Meaning

The PM Instinct occurs once the PM Mindset operates automatically. When you have developed the PM Instinct, the PMI-aligned answer is determined before you finish deliberating. You recognize the answer and understand why the other options are wrong faster than before. Your first answer is consistently correct, and you no longer doubt the answer you select. You know that you know that you know.

When you do change your answer, you think to yourself: I knew the answer I selected was right, but I was uncertain. And your instinct was correct. You did not trust it.

The signs that you have crossed into PM Instinct are equally specific. The framework, principles, and processes are no longer just a reference. They have become ingrained within your conscious and activated in your subconscious. It is something you inhabit. The PM Instinct is what 13 days of intensive pattern correction and recognition built in me. It helped me with accuracy, efficiency, speed to answer, and overall alignment to the PMI-preferred answer. The amount of material I consumed was raw input and data. The Book of Wrongs was the compression algorithm and lessons learned. The instinct was the output: a trained response system that could decipher ambiguous scenarios and arrive at PMI's preferred answer without doubting the reason why.

The difference between the PM Mindset and the PM Instinct is the difference between knowing and believing. One requires constant monitoring. The other is embedded in the behavior itself. One is conscious. The other is subconscious.

CHAPTER 5

The Three Stages of Growth

Stage 1 — PM Mindset. At this stage, the framework, processes, and principles are all understood. You know what PMI rewards and can apply it consciously: analyze before acting, lead with servant leadership, follow formal change control, protect quality, and think comprehensively. You can explain why an answer is right, even when you chose the wrong one.

This is where many candidates plateau, and where most study guides stop. The toolkit is there. But the real question is this: can you still choose the right answer when the pressure is on and you have about 1 minute and 16 seconds per question? And if you stumble, can you recover fast enough to keep going without doubt?

Stage 2 — PM Alignment. This is the stage where you create your own Book of Wrongs to correct your thinking and bring it into closer alignment with PMI's framework. You develop a concise plan to address the areas of opportunity revealed through lessons learned along the way. Every wrong answer becomes both a lesson and a reflective checkpoint, not only to identify the correct answer, but to reinforce the reasoning behind it.

This stage is uncomfortable because it requires honesty. You have to sit with your mistakes, diagnose them clearly, and rewrite the mental model that produced them. The Book of Wrongs is the tool for that work. It turns individual misses into pattern data, and pattern data into correction targets.

Stage 3 — PM Instinct. You have the mindset and the alignment. The calibration is complete to the point that recognition becomes second nature. The framework becomes a part of you. You can read a scenario and recognize the best answer before you finish reviewing every option.

When an answer is wrong, you know why it is wrong, not because you memorized past questions, but because it violates a pattern your thinking has been trained to detect. This is the stage that helps you pass and positions you to potentially score Above Target.

This is not a quick fix. It is the cumulative result of reprioritizing your backlog of life and making enough deliberate corrections that the correction itself becomes invisible.

The 5 PM Instincts

After two failed attempts and one passing attempt, I began to recognize what the exam kept rewarding. I could see the patterns. Those patterns eventually led to the development of five instincts that helped me choose the right answers consistently.

There is no fixed set of questions to memorize. What began firing automatically were trained responses built through knowledge, practice exams and quizzes, application, and a deep understanding of the PM Mindset aligned with PMI's framework. Together, those instincts became my operating system.

Every wrong answer in my Book of Wrongs eventually traced back to violating one of these instincts. That is why they matter. They are not just concepts; they are correction targets. When the same instinct keeps appearing in your misses, you have found a pattern. And when you have found a pattern, you know what needs to be corrected.

The mindset says, "I understand how PMI wants me to think."

The instinct says, "I recognize the right answer and choose it."

What follows is the decision filter. These are the five instincts I learned to run every question through.

The 5 PM Instincts — Your Decision Filter

Before selecting any answer, run it through these five instincts. They are not a checklist to rush through; they are the decision filter you apply in order. The PM Mindset helps you understand how PMI wants you to think. The PM Instinct helps you recognize the right answer and choose it under pressure.

Instinct #1 — Analyze Before You Act

Before choosing an action, make sure you understand what is actually happening. Identify the root cause, the context, the impact, and the stakeholder situation before you move. If an answer jumps straight into action without first assessing the situation, it is often the wrong choice.

Micro-example: A risk occurs during execution. The tempting answer is to update the schedule immediately. PMI wants you to first assess the impact of the risk, review the risk response plan, and understand how project objectives are affected before deciding what to do next.

Instinct #2 — Coach or Facilitate Before Escalating

Do not jump to the sponsor, senior management, or formal escalation before direct resolution has been attempted. PMI generally rewards the project manager for coaching, facilitating, collaborating, and addressing issues at the appropriate level before escalating, unless the situation clearly requires otherwise.

Micro-example: Two team members are in conflict and morale is beginning to suffer. The tempting answer is to escalate the issue to senior management. PMI wants you to first address the conflict directly through facilitation or appropriate conflict management before escalating.

Instinct #3 — Protect Compliance and Quality

Stay aligned with standards, requirements, conformance, and corrective action when quality or compliance is at risk. PMI does not reward passive observation when a deviation has already been identified. Be proactive. If a process, requirement, or standard is off track, the project manager should think in terms of correction, prevention, and control.

Micro-example: A quality audit identifies a process deviation, but no defect has occurred yet. The tempting answer is to document it and continue monitoring. PMI wants you to investigate the cause and take corrective action to bring the process back into compliance before the deviation becomes a defect.

Instinct #4 — Recognize the Methodology

Every scenario operates within a methodology: predictive, agile, or hybrid. Your answer must stay within that methodology. Governance structure, sprint language, role definitions, change processes, approval flow, and decision-making patterns are not background details. They are clues that tell you how PMI expects you to respond.

Micro-example: A sponsor requests a new feature. In a predictive environment, the request goes through formal change control. In an agile environment, it goes into the product backlog and is prioritized by the product owner. Same request. Different methodology. Different answer.

Instinct #5 — Trust Your Trained First Answer

If your PMI-aligned reasoning led you to an answer, do not override it just because anxiety shows up. Change your answer only when new reasoning or new information justifies the change. Do not let panic rewrite your preparation.

Micro-example: You choose an answer, feel confident, then reread the options and start wanting to switch. Nothing new in the question changes the logic. That is not insight; that is anxiety. PM Instinct says to trust the trained answer unless a real reason emerges to change it.

Why These 5 PM Instincts Matter

The PM Instinct is not guesswork. It is trained PMI-aligned judgment that becomes fast, reliable, and trusted under pressure. I repeat things throughout this book intentionally, because repetition is the foundation for going from mindset to alignment to instinct. Hang in there. Keep reading. These five instincts will turn the PM Mindset into a decision filter you can actually use under pressure, so that when it counts, you do not just know how PMI wants you to think. You recognize the right answer and select it.

The Frustration Phase

Frustration is a sign that you care deeply about something — passing, in this case. It can also be a sign that you are mentally worn down and closer to giving up than you want to admit. The weight of this exam can feel heavy. I had that thought myself, wondering whether the benefits outweighed the time, effort, and sacrifice. When that happens, stop. Give yourself grace. Recharge. Then come back with a renewed mind and spirit.

Because on the surface, nothing looks broken. You know change control. You know servant leadership. You know the difference between agile and predictive. But when you sit down with a scenario, something shifts. The answer feels right, until it isn't. That kind of frustration hits differently because it is not rooted in not knowing. It is rooted in the gap between what you know and how you are applying it under pressure.

I got angry with myself on more than one occasion. Not in a destructive way, but in the way you do when you know you are capable of more. The pressure was internal. Time was slipping into the future. My study partner had already passed. The shared journey was over. It was just me and the score I still had not reached.

I stopped focusing on being right and started understanding why I was wrong. Before I created the Book of Wrongs, I was already working through one of my final notebooks. I had written a lot, but I had not yet condensed what I was learning into something more usable. That changed when I stopped trying to capture everything and started identifying the PMI signals I had been overlooking in the explanations: assess impact, analyze root cause, engage stakeholders, review the risk response, follow change control, facilitate resolution, and take corrective action. Part of it was application, but with anything, you must obtain the knowledge and learn the patterns before true application can occur in a high-quality way. I also learned to read the contextual details that shaped the right answer, such as delivery approach, team maturity, contract type, governance structure, and whether a change control board was present.

Slowly, frustration turned into familiarity. I was no longer just seeing questions; I was recognizing patterns. I could tell when PMI wanted change control, when it wanted risk response, and when it wanted stakeholder communication instead of a rushed action that only looked decisive. When a specific exam task needed work, I went straight into PMI Study Hall and used it as a targeted clinic for my weakest areas. I was starting to get my makosa right.

When frustration turns into aggravation, redirect it into motivation. Sometimes you can understand the material, put in the hours, and still not break through. That tension can be a sign that you are close.

The frustration phase is like the person digging for diamonds who gives up just before breaking through. The breakthrough may be closer than it appears, but fatigue, doubt, and repetition can make it feel farther away than it really is, especially when you are also balancing family, work, and other responsibilities. Keep digging.

The Cost

The frustration phase can become either an asset or a liability, and that depends largely on your thinking. Honestly, it cost time and attention more than some will admit. Free time once spent with family, friends, and other endeavors was redirected into review sessions. Weekends became practice exam cycles. The backlog of life was reprioritized to create as much capacity as possible to pass the PMP.

The frustration hit hardest when the scores did not match the amount of time I was spending studying to pass. That gap, between effort invested and results produced, was one of the hardest parts of the process. If you know, you know.

There was a moment when I questioned whether this was something I was supposed to pursue. Doubt crept in. Then I went down memory lane and played everything back, reminding myself of all I had gone through to get to that point, and I decided: I will pass.

Failure was not an option, and I had no appetite for it. It was not on my plate.

The Reset

There were study sessions where I closed the laptop, stopped the practice exams, turned off the YouTube videos, closed the books, and put all of the PMP content away. I knew when to give myself grace and slow down to recharge. I didn't want to reinforce bad patterns instead of building better ones. Acknowledging your frustration and your need for rest is critical. Continuing without resetting is not discipline; it is repetition of the wrong thing.

You don't get better by doing more without pause. You get better by doing it right, then allowing it to settle, by thinking more clearly tomorrow than you were right then. That became a habit. Controlled reset. Not retreat. There is a difference between quitting a session and quitting the goal. One is discipline. The other is defeat. I only ever did the first.

CHAPTER 7

The 13-Day Turnaround

My first exam date was delayed and rescheduled, and the follow-up came with technical issues, distractions, and ultimately a fail. I failed my second exam. I knew I needed to try again without pushing it out any further. I paid again in both time and money. The exam was rescheduled 13 days out. I had one attempt left and less than a month to pass, or my time would expire and I would have to go through the full process again. I needed a plan, one that would actually work.

I thought the plan through, and if there is nothing else to take from this chapter, remember this: start with your exam report if you took the actual exam. If not, start with your mock score. I recommend using Study Hall. Your exam analysis will show you which tasks need review and which lessons or areas need improvement. Build from that.

Step 1 — Read the score report honestly

I gave myself a short emotional reset, then opened the score report and treated it like data. I reviewed the exam analysis thoroughly to identify the weak domains, weak tasks, and recurring patterns. That score report became the plan.

Step 2 — Write the weak tasks down and make them a checklist

Once I saw what needed improvement, I wrote those tasks down and turned them into a checklist. That gave me something clear to work from instead of studying blindly.

Step 3 — Go task by task in Study Hall

I went directly into the Study Hall lessons tied to the weak tasks. I revisited the lessons carefully, matched them to the areas I needed to improve, and used the related quizzes to see whether the gap was actually closing, instead of assuming it was.

Step 4 — Cross-reference with your main PMP book

After reviewing the Study Hall lessons, I cross-referenced them with Rita's. You can use whichever PMP book works for you. I did not reread everything. I went back only to the chapters, agile topics, and process explanations connected to the tasks the score report showed were weak.

Step 5 — Take notes and track what you missed

As I reviewed, I took notes. I wrote down what mattered, what I kept missing, and what PMI was really looking for in those task areas.

Step 6 — Quiz yourself and practice with a study partner

In the last stretch, I used 50-question timed exams every other day for a week, often with a study buddy. We answered the same questions at the same time, then compared how we each read the scenario, what PMI behavior we saw, and why one answer was stronger than another. Those every-other-day sessions over about 10 days sharpened my mindset and helped convert it into instinct faster than solo review ever did.

What made the turnaround work was sequence: score report first, weak task next, lesson and quiz after that, book chapter review where needed, then final consolidation into the Book of Wrongs. That sequence turned mindset into instinct.

Step 7 — Use the last 3 days to build the Book of Wrongs

In the final 3 days, the Book of Wrongs took its final form. Only after the task-by-task review, cross-referencing, notes, quizzes, timed every-other-day practice, and study-partner comparison did I consolidate everything. I pulled wrong answers from mocks, minis, quizzes, and notes, then organized them by principle, process, domain, and mindset error. The Book of Wrongs was the final consolidation step, not the starting point.

Book of Wrongs

The Book of Wrongs, as stated before, is called Kitabu Cha Makosa, which is Swahili for "Book of Wrongs." Within it, you create your own Table of Contents, and then build it in this order:

1. PM Mindset principles written out in your own understanding and words.

2. PM Alignment: all 49 processes written out.

3. A one-hour PM Mindset/PM Alignment YouTube video of your choice that covers the PMP, with you taking notes the entire time.

4. Exam and quiz review focused on your wrong answers, writing out why the correct answers are correct, not to memorize them, but to understand how they are correct.

5. PM Mindset principles written out again, updated based on what you've learned.

6. PM Alignment: the 49 processes written out again.

7. PM Instinct written out in your own words, including how your thinking and decision-making have changed.

The Purpose of the Book of Wrongs

After my second failure, I had notebooks full of notes. Process charts. Videos watched twice. I had done the volume. The scores were not moving. The problem was not effort. The problem was that I was consuming more content and trying to remember what I got wrong without correcting my thinking. I was restating misses, not diagnosing them. Every review session ended with, "I'll remember that next time," but next time the same pattern showed up wearing a different scenario.

The Book of Wrongs was built to solve a deeper problem. It was not just about asking, "What did I miss?" It was about asking, "What did PMI expect here?" From there, it became a way to build the PM Mindset, strengthen the right PM Alignment, and sharpen what I call PM Instinct, while reinforcing the foundational areas required to pass the PMP. It forced me to stop treating wrong answers like isolated mistakes and start reading them as evidence of how I was thinking.

That was the paradigm shift. The Book of Wrongs was not just a place to record missed questions. It became the final tool I used to instill the right thinking needed to pass the PMP. It helped me identify patterns, correct them, and reinforce the principles behind them. Once I started using it that way, wrong answers stopped feeling like individual failures and started feeling like data. The shift was from passive review to active diagnosis. A wrong answer is not just a missed question. It is evidence of a thinking pattern that will continue to produce wrong answers unless the pattern itself is identified, corrected, and reinforced.

Timing Is Everything

The Book of Wrongs, in its final consolidated form, was built during the last 3 days. Give yourself grace and understand that this process is case by case. Some people may be able to build their Book of Wrongs in the last 5 days, but I would say the minimum should be 3 focused days to really get your makosa right.

The day before the exam, you should review your own Book of Wrongs so that your corrections, patterns, and PMI thinking are fresh in your mind. Timing was not accidental. Going through the 13-Day Turnaround from Step 1 through Step 7 was critical because it made the Book of Wrongs intentional, not random.

What made it effective was not just writing down wrong answers at the end. It was the sequence behind it. Each step built on the one before it. By the time I reached the final days, I was not starting from scratch. I was consolidating lessons, patterns, weak areas, and corrected thinking into one place. That is what gave the Book of Wrongs its power.

All of the notebooks I filled with PMP notes were useful, but there was way too much information to go back through. The problem was not effort or lack of material. The problem was that the information was too broad, too scattered, and not organized around the patterns that were actually costing me points. The system did not become powerful until it was built in sequence: score report first, then weak task identification, then task-level Study Hall lessons, and finally Book of Wrongs consolidation. That sequence is what transforms a collection of missed questions into a calibration tool.

Getting My Makosa Right: Real Book of Wrongs Entries

What finally changed for me was not more notes. It was correcting the notes I already had. I stopped treating wrong answers like random misses and started treating them like evidence of how I was thinking.

These were the kinds of corrections that began showing up in my Book of Wrongs — Kitabu Cha Makosa (Swahili for "Book of Wrongs"). This is what getting my makosa — my mistakes — right looked like in practice.

Makosa #1 — Risk vs. Change Control

Makosa: Risk response requires a change request.

Correction: Not always. A risk is a future uncertainty, and responses can be handled within the approved plan or with contingency reserve. A change request is required when the response impacts an approved baseline or requires management reserve.

Makosa #2 — Stakeholders vs. Escalation

Makosa: Escalate stakeholder issues quickly.

Correction: PMI rewards engagement before escalation. The project manager should first assess, communicate, and facilitate resolution at the appropriate level. Escalate only when authority, governance, or risk thresholds are exceeded.

Makosa #3 — Agile Misunderstanding

Makosa: Include all stakeholders in sprint planning.

Correction: Agile requires targeted stakeholder engagement, not broad inclusion. The right stakeholders are involved at the right time through defined roles, not at every ceremony.

Makosa #4 — PM Authority

Makosa: The project manager makes the decisions.

Correction: The PM leads and facilitates decisions but does not own all of them. The team owns technical execution. The sponsor and governance bodies handle decisions beyond project authority.

Makosa #5 — Methodology Recognition

Makosa: Agile, predictive, and hybrid are just concepts to know.

Correction: They are behavior signals. Predictive uses baselines and formal change control. Agile uses backlogs and iterative delivery. Hybrid requires knowing which governance layer applies before acting.

Makosa #6 — Estimation and Planning

Makosa: If estimating is difficult, move forward and adjust later.

Correction: Difficulty estimating is a signal to increase clarity. Break the work down, use expert judgment, historical data, and assumptions before committing to unreliable estimates.

Makosa #7 — Contracts and Uncertainty

Makosa: Fixed-price contracts are generally the best option.

Correction: Contract selection depends on uncertainty. Fixed-price fits well-defined scope. Time and materials fits flexible effort. Cost-reimbursable fits high uncertainty and shifts more risk to the buyer.

The Shift

This was the difference.

My notes stopped being a collection of information and started becoming calibration. I was no longer just writing down what I got wrong. I was identifying the thinking pattern behind the miss, correcting it, and turning it into something I could carry into the next question.

That is what the Book of Wrongs became.

Not a notebook. A correction system.

Book of Wrongs Entry Templates

Use one of the two templates below as your starting format. The Quick-Entry template is for your first pass; the Comprehensive template is for deeper diagnosis.

Quick-Entry Template

Topic / question type: ___

Domain: ___ | Task area: ___ | Keywords I missed: ___

My answer and why it felt right: ___

PMI's answer (in my own words): ___

The gap — what PMI wanted that I missed: ___

Instinct tag / correction rule: ___

Which PM Instinct(s) this miss violated: ___

Comprehensive Template

Question / scenario: ___ | Domain: People / Process / Business Environment | Task: ___

What I chose: ___ | Why it looked right: ___

Keywords or clues I missed: ___ | What made PMI's answer right: ___

Relevant process / principle / agile behavior: ___ | What I will do next time: ___

Which PM Instinct(s) this miss violated: ___

Optional — PMBOK 7 Principle: ___ | Performance Domain: ___ | Life Cycle Context: Predictive / Agile / Hybrid

Why the wrong answer felt right (trap pattern in one sentence): ___

A Note on Longer Windows

The 13-Day Turnaround is what I used. It was built from necessity. Thirteen days was what I had. If your situation gives you more time, here is how I would approach a 30-day window using the same principles that made the turnaround work.

The 30-Day Push

Weeks 1–2: Deep dive into your Book of Wrongs. No new question banks. Only review of documented patterns, missed tasks, and principle violations. Rewrite key mindset principles daily.

Week 3: Targeted Study Hall lessons for the three task areas that kept appearing in your Book of Wrongs. Watch lessons with the book open, annotating entries with new insights.

Week 4: 50-question timed exams every other day. Review with a study buddy where possible to compare mindset, logic, and why one PMI answer beat another. After each set: pattern review first, then score.

Final 3 days: No new material. Only Book of Wrongs review, principle review, and rest. Watch fatigue carefully. When a streak of right answers suddenly becomes a streak of wrong ones, treat that as a conditioning signal, not a character flaw.

CHAPTER 8

The Breakthrough

Breakthroughs did not come from hope alone, but from doing the work, trusting the process, and staying resilient through every obstacle and setback. There was a time when quizzes, mock exams, and the exam itself held more uncertainty than certainty, but that changed. As I developed the PM Mindset, aligned with PMI's way of thinking, and honed the PM Instinct, I began to trust my first trained answer, and more of those answers were correct. My scores improved. I could see when a question was really about change control, even if it never said "change request." I could tell when PMI wanted me to pause and communicate instead of act, even when the situation sounded urgent. I could feel when a scenario called for a predictive response versus an agile one, and when hybrid meant honoring both. The same exam that once felt like a blur of possibilities became a finite set of consistent, repeatable moves. I was no longer facing 180 isolated questions. I was seeing variations of a mindset I had finally learned to speak.

PM Mindset vs. PM Instinct

There is a distinction I want to be precise about, because it explains what the breakthrough actually is. The PM

Mindset is the toolkit: the language, the processes, the domains, and the frameworks that help you think the way PMI expects. It is what you build when you study. Mindset teaches you what change control is, what servant leadership means, the difference between product scope and project scope, and what the risk register is for. Every candidate who passes eventually acquires the PM Mindset. But acquiring it does not guarantee that you can use it correctly under pressure.

The PM Instinct is what happens when that toolkit becomes internalized. It is no longer something you consult; it is something you operate from. It is the trained ability to recognize the shape of the right answer under pressure without having to reason through every option from scratch. You read a scenario and something in you already knows the PMI-aligned move before doubt has time to interfere.

The PM Mindset is built through study, structure, and understanding. The PM Instinct is built through repetition, correction, and enough deliberate practice that the right response begins to fire automatically.

The PM Mindset helps you recognize what the question is asking. The PM Instinct helps you recognize the answer, with greater speed, clarity, and confidence.

The Driving Analogy

Think about the first time you learned to drive. Every action was deliberate: check the mirror, signal, check the blind spot, ease off the brake, apply pressure gradually. You were not bad at driving. You were simply at the mindset stage. You knew what to do, but you had not yet built the habit of doing it automatically.

After enough practice, driving stopped requiring active thought. You did not stop at every sign and recite the rules. You responded. The knowledge had become reflex.

The PMP is similar. Studying PMI processes, principles, and question patterns builds the mindset. Reviewing wrong answers, correcting patterns, and using the Book of Wrongs trains the instinct. At some point, the right PMI-aligned answer starts showing up before you finish reading the scenario. That shift is the breakthrough.

On exam day you are sharper, steadier, and more confident. Not because the exam got easier, but because your thinking did. That is what Above Target begins to look like in practice.

CHAPTER 9

Recognize the Methodology

Of the five PM Instincts introduced in Chapter 5, Instinct #4 — Recognize the Methodology — was the one that cost me the most points before I truly understood what it required. It was not enough to know that agile and predictive existed. I had to recognize which one I was operating inside before I could answer correctly.

For a long time, one of the consistent sources of wrong answers in my Book of Wrongs was the agile versus predictive distinction. Not because I did not know the definitions. I could recite them. The problem was that I was mixing up the behaviors.

The true distinction for me came down to the signals in the scenario and to how much of the work was being defined up front. In a predictive environment, scope and planning tend to be more stable and front-loaded, with baselines, formal approvals, and change control guiding the work. In an agile environment, the work is refined iteratively through backlogs, feedback loops, reviews, and retrospectives, with the team adapting as learning emerges. In a hybrid environment, both patterns may appear.

Looking for keywords became one of my most reliable tools. Predictive scenarios often signal themselves through language like baseline, formal approval, change control board, and scheduled review. Agile scenarios often signal themselves through language like sprint, product backlog, retrospective, and self-organizing team. Once I trained myself to spot those signals first, the right behavior followed more naturally.

One additional insight that helped me was recognizing that feasibility and other front-end analysis often signaled a more predictive orientation. That connection helped me enter the scenario from the right starting point instead of the wrong one.

Agile meant self-organizing teams, iterative delivery, backlog refinement, frequent stakeholder feedback, and adapting as new information emerged. Predictive meant baselines, formal change control, scheduled reviews, and more structured approval and escalation paths. What kept costing me points was applying agile behavior to predictive scenarios and predictive behavior to agile ones.

The shift happened when I stopped asking, What framework is this? and started asking, What behavior does this environment call for? What keywords or cues does the scenario give me? The scenario tells you. You just have to be trained to read it.

Once I separated the behaviors, the pattern recognition accelerated. That one correction improved my accuracy across both the Process and People domains.

Life-Cycle Selection Is Driven by Uncertainty and Change, Not Preference

The scenario tells you which life cycle to use. High requirement uncertainty and frequent stakeholder feedback loops point toward agile. Stable, well-defined requirements with a fixed budget and sequential dependencies point toward predictive. Hybrid is chosen when different workstreams have different profiles.

The wrong answer is usually the one that picks a life cycle based on team familiarity or convenience rather than the project's actual risk and change profile. PMI rewards the PM who reads the environment and selects accordingly, not the one who defaults to what is comfortable.

Agile Reality Checks

After that shift clicked, I went deeper into the Agile Practice Guide. Worth noting: PMI members get access to the Agile Practice Guide and the PMBOK guides at no additional cost. If you have not joined as a member yet, that access alone can justify the fee.

What I found in the Agile Practice Guide was not definitions. I already had those. What I found was a set of behaviors the exam keeps testing at the execution level. These were the ones I kept getting wrong because I understood the concept but not what it actually looked like under exam pressure.

Servant leadership is active, not passive. PMI's agile PM does not simply get out of the team's way. They actively remove impediments, facilitate retrospectives, resolve ambiguity, protect the team from outside interruptions, and ensure the team has what it needs to self-direct. Passive noninterference is a trap answer. Active facilitation and coaching is almost always right.

Self-managing teams still need coaching and clarity. A self-managing team owns the how. The PM owns the why, the what, and the environment. When a self-managing team hits an unclear requirement or a process breakdown, the PM steps in with coaching and boundary clarification, not control, but not absence either. If the scenario shows a self-managing team stuck or confused, the PM engages. That is not micromanagement. That is servant leadership.

Retrospectives are improvement engines, not ceremony. If a scenario involves a team that keeps making the same mistakes, the answer almost always involves the retrospective, or the lack of one. PMI expects retrospectives to drive real process change, not just produce a document. If the team is not improving, the retrospective is not working.

Hybrid work requires deliberate translation between worlds. In a hybrid environment, some workstreams follow predictive governance and others follow agile self-organization. The PM's job is to translate between those worlds, not to apply one approach everywhere. Metrics, status reporting, and change management look different on each side. Translating them deliberately, not forcing standardization, is what PMI rewards.

Hybrid Scenarios — The Exam's Sharpest Trap

This is where most of the advanced wrong answers live. Hybrid scenarios test whether you can hold two governance layers simultaneously, and know which one applies to the decision in front of you.

Rule 1 — Don't force predictive change control into clearly agile team decisions. If the team is self-managing and the decision lives entirely within the sprint, the team owns it. The product owner manages the backlog. A PM who routes internal sprint-level decisions through a change control board is applying the wrong governance layer.

Rule 2 — Don't ignore governance because delivery is agile. The agile team governs the work. The contract and organizational governance govern the project. A new requirement that expands contracted scope still requires a formal change request, regardless of how the team is delivering. Agile delivery does not dissolve contractual accountability.

Rule 3 — Translate metrics across workstreams; don't standardize them blindly. A hybrid project may have a predictive phase measured by EVM and an agile phase measured by velocity. The PM's job is to translate and communicate both in terms the sponsor can understand, not to force one measurement approach onto both sides.

Rule 4 — Respect both the governance boundary and the team autonomy boundary simultaneously. The team has autonomy over how they work. The organization has authority over what gets approved and contracted. A PM who dictates sprint decisions violates team autonomy. A PM who lets the team scope-creep past contracted boundaries violates governance. The exam tests whether you can hold both at once.

Hybrid trap in one sentence: You are operating in two governance layers at the same time. Know which layer the decision belongs to before you act.

What Recognizing the Methodology Actually Does

Instinct #4 is not just about knowing the difference between agile and predictive. It is about reading the environment the scenario gives you — the keywords, the governance structure, the team setup, the change process — and letting those signals tell you which behavior PMI expects before you evaluate a single answer option.

When this instinct is developed, the methodology stops being something you identify after reading the question. It becomes something you recognize before you finish the first sentence. The scenario tells you where you are. Your job is to be trained enough to hear it.

That is what Recognize the Methodology means in practice. Not a definition. A trained read.

CHAPTER 10

The Pass

I told a lot of people about how I was taking the PMP exam, how much time and dedication it took. When the second attempt came and I failed, I went silent. I was too embarrassed and disappointed in myself to break the news to anyone. I told everyone I would rather not discuss anything related to the PMP until I simply passed. No updates. No conversations. Just silence and work.

The third attempt was scheduled 13 days later at an OnVue location. The night before, I found myself up periodically, going through the Book of Wrongs and reviewing questions with one of my study partners. Not out of panic. Out of preparation. That was the difference.

I took the exam. When I walked out to receive my results, I told the woman at the desk I did not want to look. She encouraged me to take a look anyway. I did. Above Target in all three domains: People, Process, and Business Environment. Since my body could not do it, my spirit did a backflip. My smile said everything.

I passed.

The exam was not a walk in the park. There were screwball questions, scenarios where three answers all looked like they could be right and nothing felt obvious. But where the material made sense, I was able to pull from my mental information bank and draw from the PM Mindset and PM Alignment I had built. And where the pressure increased and the answers all looked equally plausible, the PM Instinct took over. Not guessing. Drawing from trained pattern recognition.

That is what the system produced. Not a perfect exam. A prepared mind that could navigate an imperfect one.

I think about the candidates who are one attempt away from passing and do not know it. People who are so close that the gap is not knowledge but thinking. Not effort but direction. If there is one thing I want you to take from this chapter, it is this: you are probably closer than you think. The wall is not a wall. It is a direction correction.

The same score report that once highlighted my Process weakness now read like a different story. The numbers did not change because I found a secret shortcut or a magic resource. They changed because my thinking did.

I walked out of that testing center knowing I had not just answered differently. I had become someone different in the way I approached every scenario. The project was complete. The deliverable was in hand. But the real result was the mindset I now carried into every project, every decision, and every conversation.

What Above Target in All Domains Actually Means

There are four possible results for each domain: Needs Improvement, Below Target, Target, and Above Target. In my experience, many passing reports cluster around Target in most domains, with Above Target in at least one. Exact patterns vary by candidate and exam form. Hitting Above Target across all three means your thinking was consistently aligned with PMI's expectations regardless of question type. It does not mean you answered every question correctly. It means your decision-making framework was PMI's framework.

That is what the Book of Wrongs builds. Not a collection of memorized answers. A retrained way of thinking that holds up under pressure, across all three domains, in 180 different scenarios.

> *"The PMP is not a test of what you know. It is a test of how you think and what you know. When your thinking aligns with PMI's, the answers follow." — Cartraill Love*

CHAPTER 11

Reviewing Your Score Report(s)

At a practical level, People focuses on leadership, communication, stakeholder engagement, and team dynamics. Process focuses on planning and delivery across scope, value, resources, procurement, finance, quality, schedule, status, and closure. Business Environment focuses on governance, compliance, change, risk, and the broader organizational context around the project. Candidates should always interpret their score reports against the active ECO for their exam date, not just against older advice or prior versions of the test.

It should be noted that the domain percentages referenced in this chapter reflect both the exam structure I prepared under and my own practical blueprint based on what did and did not work during my attempts. My interpretation is drawn from lived experience, not official PMI scoring language.

Under PMI's 2021 Examination Content Outline (ECO), which was in effect when I sat for the exam, the domains were weighted as People 42%, Process 50%, and Business Environment 8%. Under the 2026 ECO that PMI has announced for the exam version planned to start in July 2026, the domains are reweighted to People 33%, Process 41%, and Business Environment 26%. PMI also notes that about 40% of the exam will reflect predictive approaches, while the remaining 60% will be divided between adaptive/agile and hybrid approaches across all three domains.

That change matters. Candidates testing from July 2026 forward should not rely only on the older 42/50/8 model, especially because Business Environment becomes much more significant in the new outline. In the updated ECO, that domain includes governance, compliance, change control, issue and impediment management, risk, continuous improvement, organizational change, and changes in the external business environment.

Always confirm the active ECO and domain weights on PMI's official site before you finalize your study plan, especially if your exam date is near a change window.

With the July 2026 exam update, it would also be wise to review the PMBOK 8th Edition. I have included an overview in the appendices for those interested.

Decoding Tasks and Domains

If you scored lower than expected, or even failed, begin with every task or area marked Needs Improvement or Below Target. Determine what those tasks are really testing. Then identify the resources that can help you strengthen them, whether that is books, Study Hall, YouTube, or other trusted tools. Take notes as you review, and if necessary, say those notes out loud until the concepts, patterns, and PMI logic start to settle into place.

After a failed attempt or a score lower than expected, work through these questions honestly:

- Which domain is Below Target? Start there. Do not divide your energy evenly if one domain is clearly pulling your result down.

- Within that domain, which tasks were scored? Use Study Hall's task-level data to identify the specific task statements that remain consistently weak.

- If Process is weak, is the problem broad or concentrated? For example, are you struggling across the domain, or mainly in areas such as executing or monitoring and controlling? That distinction should shape your study strategy.

- If People is weak, what kind of misses are happening? Are they tied more to leadership style, stakeholder engagement, escalation, or conflict handling? Those require different corrections.

A score report should never be treated as a disappointment alone. It is a diagnostic tool. Read it carefully, and it will tell you where to focus, what to correct, and how to prepare differently the next time.

Targeted Correction, Don't Restart

When some candidates receive a failed exam result, their instinct is to start over: re-read all the chapters, review all the resources, and redo the same questions to remember them. I am not saying you should never review. I am saying the goal should be efficiency and focus. A broad restart treats the entire journey as the problem when your score report is showing you something specific.

If you restart the full process instead of targeting the areas marked Needs Improvement and Below Target, you risk spending time on what is already working while the real gaps stay untouched. You have a better chance of strengthening those weak areas, maintaining your stronger areas, and improving across all domains when you study with precision.

This is where PMI Study Hall becomes especially helpful. If you are using the learning plan, it will show you an overview of your strengths and weaknesses across domains and tasks. The Strengths and Weaknesses view shows your proficiency in a category based on both your answers and the difficulty of the questions. The learning plan then breaks down core information task by task so you can target and improve exactly where needed. The mock exams also include a report section that shows your score history and trends for each task area. I used Study Hall as a critical resource and everything else as cross-reference and expansion points.

The correct strategy is targeted correction, not a broad restart.

Here is the approach that worked for me:

- Identify: Find the 3–5 task areas in your weakest domain with Below Target or mid-range performance. Be specific. Not just "Process is weak," but "Change Control and Risk Response within Process are weak."

- Isolate: Go into PMI Study Hall and review the lessons specifically for those task areas, not the full domain review. Focus on the task-level lessons.

- Extract: For each lesson, pull the key insight into your Book of Wrongs. Link it to an existing wrong-answer pattern you have already documented.

- Reinforce: Use Prepsaret or another trusted question bank for targeted questions in that task area only. Do not spread into new areas until the targeted task shows clear improvement.

- Supplement Strategically: Once the targeted area is stable, bring in other resources with intention. PMBOK 7 for principles, Rita for process flow, and David McLachlan for concepts that may not click through text alone.

This is not about doing less work. It is about doing the right work. Targeted correction compounds. Broad studying dilutes.

My Specific Pattern, and What It Taught Me

After my first failure (March 2025), my score report showed Process Below Target with People and Business Environment at Target. I treated it like feedback on a performance instead of a roadmap. After my second failure (March 2026), my progress seemingly diminished with Process rated as Needs Improvement, but now I understood what it meant. Process was still the domain holding me back, which confirmed that my real-world instincts were overriding PMI's structured approach on execution and monitoring questions. I was answering based on what I would do, not what PMI expects.

The correction was not more questions. It was going back through the lessons tied to my areas of opportunity, rebuilding my mental map of the project flow, and drilling the change control and risk response patterns through my Book of Wrongs until they became automatic. On my third attempt (March 17, 2026), Process went to Above Target. Not because the questions changed. Because my thinking did. I had not only developed the PM Mindset, but aligned with PMI's framework deeply enough for the PM Instinct to take over under pressure.

If your exam is 30–45 days away, apply the same recovery principles from the 13-Day Turnaround at a slower pace: start with your score report or mock results, identify your weakest task areas, review them with your strongest resources, consolidate the patterns into your Book of Wrongs, and finish with final mock review.

CHAPTER 12

From Student to Mentor

During my journey to obtain the PMP, I connected with others. We studied together. We held sessions. They passed. I realized something valuable: I did not just obtain my PMP. I became someone who could help other people navigate the same resistance, the same noise, the same frustration, and the same turning point I faced. That shift from student to mentor is available to anyone who completes this journey. But it requires a conscious decision to use what you have learned to pull others forward, not for status or self-gain, but for purpose and humanity.

How to Help Another Candidate

If someone comes to you after a failed attempt, or while they are still struggling through mock exams and quizzes, do not start by handing them more resources. Start by understanding where the breakdown is occurring. This is the framework I would use:

Step 1 — Ask for the score report or mock exam results.

Start with the data. If they have taken the actual exam, review the score report. If they have not, review their mock exam and quiz results. Look at domain performance, task-level patterns, and recurring misses to identify the clearest areas of opportunity.

Step 2 — Ask about their study method.

Are they reviewing their wrong answers in detail, or just moving on? Are they studying with intention, or simply consuming more material and taking more questions? This helps reveal whether the issue is content knowledge, process, mindset, or a combination of all three.

Step 3 — Explain what is really required to pass.

Help them understand that passing the PMP is not only about obtaining knowledge. It also requires developing the PM Mindset, aligning that mindset with PMI's framework, and training that alignment deeply enough for the PM Instinct to begin taking shape under pressure. If they do not understand that, they may continue studying hard without correcting the way they think.

Step 4 — Identify the pattern.

Before suggesting any major adjustment, determine what is consistently happening. Are they rushing to action? Missing methodology cues? Struggling to think in a PMI-aligned way? Name the pattern before trying to correct it.

Step 5 — Strengthen the right areas first.

Use targeted review to reinforce the task areas, concepts, and mindset gaps that continue to appear. The goal at this stage is not to restart everything. It is to correct what is actually costing them points.

Step 6 — Introduce the Book of Wrongs at the right time.

If they are within 30 to 45 days of the exam, introduce the Book of Wrongs as a tool for consolidation, correction, and pattern recognition. By that point, they should have enough data, enough exposure, and enough understanding for it to become useful rather than overwhelming. If they are within 15 days of the exam, the Book of Wrongs becomes even more critical, especially for an accelerated recovery like the 13-Day Turnaround. At that stage, it should serve as a focused system for correcting patterns, sharpening PMI-aligned thinking, and reinforcing what matters most.

Step 7 — Create accountability.

Set weekly check-ins around what they are learning from missed questions, not just what they scored. The better question is not, "What did you get?" It is, "What did you correct?"

Forming a Study Group the Right Way

Ideally, two is better than one, and three is just enough to expand perspectives without creating unnecessary noise. In the PMP bootcamp, I learned that while larger groups can be helpful for networking and shared exposure, they can also introduce confusion. One person may say the questions do not make sense, even when they do make sense to you. Over time, that kind of conflict can cause you to second-guess your logic and your learning.

A PMP bootcamp can be beneficial, but whether you have taken one or not, the structure of your study group matters. If you are building or refining a small group, use the following approach:

Session 1 — Start With the Study Experience

Each person shares their PMP study experience so far: their scores, the resources they have used, what has helped, what has not, and what their score report or mock results reveal as areas needing the most improvement. The goal of this first session is not to jump into questions, but to analyze the patterns collectively and understand where each person is breaking from PMI's framework.

Session 2 — Compare Resources and Target the Right Areas

Each person identifies one resource that has genuinely helped them and explains why it has worked. They should also be honest about what has not worked. From there, everyone selects one area of opportunity to target before the next session. The point is not to collect more resources, but to identify what is useful and apply it with intention.

Session 3 — Group Review Through Targeted Questions

Before the session, each person completes 15 to 20 targeted questions in their weakest area. During the session, the group reviews the missed questions together, discusses why PMI's answer is better, and identifies where doubt, hesitation, or misalignment showed up. This is where the group begins turning mistakes into lessons learned instead of repeated misses.

Session 4 and Onward — Build Accountability and Introduce the Book of Wrongs at the Right Time

As exam dates get closer, each person should continue studying independently during the week while using the group for accountability and review. Once candidates are within the right window, especially 30 to 45 days out, or within 15 days for a turnaround push, each person should begin sharing 2 to 3 entries from their Book of Wrongs each week. At that stage, it is also important to remind one another that passing the PMP is not only about knowledge. It requires developing the PM Mindset, aligning that mindset with PMI's framework, and training that alignment deeply enough for the PM Instinct to begin taking shape under pressure. The group should then identify the mindset pattern behind each miss so everyone learns from one person's mistake.

The PMP Is More Than a Credential

The credential opens doors. But the process of earning it changes how you think. If you used the Book of Wrongs system honestly, you did not just prepare for an exam. You trained yourself to think in a more PMI-aligned way.

When a change request comes in, you evaluate impact before approving.

When a team member is struggling, you coach before you reassign.

When a risk materializes, you assess before you react.

When a stakeholder disengages, you investigate before you document.

Passing the exam was the deliverable. The Book of Wrongs became the lessons learned. Who you became in the process was the true outcome.

Now lead from that place.

APPENDIX A

PM Mindset, PM Alignment, and PM Instinct Quick Reference

How to Use This Appendix

Use this appendix as a daily PMP warm-up, a conditioning tool during practice, and a final review reference before the exam. Do not just read it silently. Read it out loud and ask yourself: Which of these did I violate yesterday or today? That question matters, because wrong answers are often the result of violated principles, not missing intelligence.

The goal is not just to memorize these instincts. The goal is to recognize when you are violating them, correct the pattern, and strengthen your PM Mindset, PM Alignment, and PM Instinct over time.

PM Response Order

This is one of the most powerful elimination tools in the book. Every question you read, run it through this order before touching the answer choices. PMI often rewards the answer that moves through this sequence instead of skipping steps.

When you are unsure which answer PMI prefers, use this decision ladder from top to bottom:

1. Assess or analyze the situation first

2. Engage the relevant stakeholders

3. Consult the plan and relevant project documents

4. Apply the process

5. Document the outcome

6. Escalate if necessary

If an answer jumps straight to escalation without evidence that the situation was assessed, the right people were engaged, or the appropriate process was considered, it is often a trap.

Instinct #1 — Analyze Before You Act

Discuss. Investigate. Determine the root cause. Review. Assess. Be proactive. Consult the right stakeholders and keep them engaged from initiation through closing. Make sure you understand the problem before you move. Do not be reactive.

Purpose in project management: Protect the project from impulsive decisions made without full information. Reactive project managers often create more cost, confusion, and rework than careful ones. Miscommunication, lack of communication, or failure to identify and engage stakeholders throughout the project life cycle can increase risk, delay, and cost.

Key words / Triggers:

> First • Next • Most appropriate • Before taking action
>
> Assess impact • Review • Investigate • Determine root cause • Analyze • Evaluate • Understand • Identify • Confirm
>
> Consult stakeholders • Engage stakeholders • Review the plan • Review the risk register • Lessons learned

Rule: If the answer skips analysis and jumps straight to action, it is likely wrong.

Instinct #2 — Coach or Facilitate Before Escalating

Lead the way PMI expects by coaching, facilitating, and resolving issues at the appropriate level before escalating. Use escalation when it is necessary and justified, not as your first move.

Purpose in project management: Team performance, trust, and sustainable output, not just short-term compliance.

Key words / Triggers:

> Team member • Conflict • Motivation • Servant leader
>
> Facilitate • Coach • Mentor • Collaborate • Empower • Support the team
>
> Resolve conflict • Meet with team member • Address directly • Active listening
>
> Remove impediments • Build consensus • Psychological safety
>
> Escalate as a last resort

Rule: Resolve at the lowest level first before escalating.

Instinct #3 — Protect Compliance and Quality

Protect quality, standards, and compliance before failure grows. When a deviation appears, do not ignore it. Investigate it. Correct it. Prevent it from becoming a larger issue. Think in terms of conformance, corrective action, and control.

Purpose in project management: Protect deliverables, processes, and outcomes from preventable defects, nonconformance, and risk exposure. PMI rewards proactive correction, not passive observation.

Key words / Triggers:

> Quality • Compliance • Standard • Audit • Deviation • Corrective action

> Nonconformance • Defect • Variance • Inspection • Quality audit

> Control quality • Manage quality • Conformance • Requirements • Regulatory

> Root cause analysis • Prevent recurrence • Update process

Rule: If a problem exists, investigate and correct it rather than monitor and wait.

Instinct #4 — Recognize the Methodology

Identify whether the environment is predictive, agile, or hybrid before deciding what to do. Look for the signals in the scenario: governance, roles, sprint language, change control, backlog use, approvals, and delivery style. The methodology is not background detail; it determines the right behavior.

Purpose in project management: Keep your response aligned with the environment the project is actually operating in. Wrong answers often come from applying the wrong behavior to the wrong methodology.

Key words / Triggers:

> Agile signals: Sprint • Backlog • Iteration • Increment • Retrospective • Daily standup • User story • Refinement • Product owner • Self-managing team • Velocity • Adaptive

> Predictive signals: Change request • CCB • Baseline • Scope baseline • Formal approval • Project management plan • Sign-off • Variance analysis • Sequential

> Hybrid signals: Hybrid • Governance • Contract • Mixed approach • Tailor • Agile delivery with formal oversight • Multiple workstreams

> Rule: If the methodology is wrong, the answer is wrong.

Instinct #5 — Trust Your Trained First Answer

If your PMI-aligned reasoning led you to an answer, do not change it just because anxiety shows up. Change your answer only when new reasoning or new information justifies the change. Do not let panic override preparation.

Purpose in project management: Protect decision quality under pressure. This instinct helps turn preparation into execution by reducing self-sabotage, hesitation, and avoidable second-guessing.

Self-check cues:

> Doubt • Second-guessing • Overthinking

No new information • No new reasoning

Anxiety • Urge to change answer

Rereading changed nothing • Stick with logic

Change only if misread • Change only if new evidence appears

Clarification: These cues do not come from the scenario. They come from your internal response to the scenario while answering.

Rule: If there is no new logic or information, do not change your answer.

Universal PMI Triggers

Strong answer signals: Assess • Analyze • Review • Identify • Facilitate • Discuss • Collaborate • Engage • Communicate • Evaluate impact • Update

Trap answer signals: Immediately escalate • Replace team member • Ignore for now • Do nothing • Act without analysis • Skip process • Blame • Punish • Jump to sponsor too early • Make unilateral decision

Context Quick Rules

In predictive: if an approved baseline is affected, formal change control is generally required, even if the change looks small.

In agile: the team owns how the work gets done, the product owner owns value and prioritization, and the project manager or agile leader facilitates, supports, and removes impediments.

In hybrid: honor the governance framework where the predictive portions require it, and honor self-organization where the agile portions require it. Do not apply the wrong control model to the wrong part of the work.

Escalation is usually a last resort, not an early reflex. Try the appropriate direct path first unless the issue clearly belongs at a higher level because of authority, governance, compliance, safety, legal exposure, or risk severity.

Stakeholder disengagement is a real project risk. Treat it with urgency based on its likely impact on decisions, delivery, value, and adoption.

Any answer that bypasses stakeholders, skips analysis, or ignores governance is often wrong.

APPENDIX B

Tools I Used: Resources

I used many resources throughout my PMP journey. I am not affiliated with any of the tools or materials I mention here. My recommendations are based only on what genuinely helped me go from two failures to passing the PMP with Above Target in all three domains.

PMI Membership + Included Guides

PMI membership mattered because it gave me access to the PMBOK Guide, the Agile Practice Guide, and other PMI standards and digital resources. That mattered to me because I wanted access to PMI's own language, principles, and framework, not just outside interpretations of them.

Whenever I needed to confirm a definition, principle, or concept, I treated PMI's materials as the source of truth. That helped keep me aligned with the way PMI expects project managers to think.

PMI Study Hall

Although it is a separate purchase, PMI Study Hall was one of the most valuable tools I used. It gave me full-length mock exams, mini exams, lessons, and quizzes tied to actual PMP tasks. More importantly, it gave me feedback.

That feedback was critical.

Study Hall helped me see where I was really strong, where I was weak, and whether I was actually improving or just feeling more confident. The task-level reporting helped me stop studying broadly and start studying with direction.

This is the official PMI practice environment, and in my experience, the wording and style of the questions felt close to the actual exam. Use it heavily. But do not just answer questions and move on. Review the explanations. Study your weaker task areas. Revisit the lessons tied to those areas. Use the tool to train your thinking, not just to chase scores.

Also, do not expect exact question repeats on the real exam. That is the wrong mindset. Question banks are for sharpening judgment, pattern recognition, and PMI-aligned decision-making.

Rita Mulcahy's PMP Exam Prep

I received Rita's book through my PMP bootcamp, and it played a major role in helping me pass. What helped me most were Rita's charts, both predictive and agile. They gave structure to the material in a way that reading alone did not.

I wrote those charts out by hand until the flows started sticking. That repetition helped me retain the material and better understand where scenarios lived in the project life cycle.

Whenever Study Hall exposed a weak task area, I would go back to the related section in Rita's and reinforce it there.

That combination kept me focused instead of scattered. Rita's helped me understand the flow, the structure, and the logic behind what PMI was testing.

Prepsaret

I came across Prepsaret through PMP groups and conversations about what prep tools were actually worth using. People kept bringing it up, and once I used it more intentionally, I understood why.

What made it valuable for me was not just the question bank. It was the way I used it.

This was one of the places where studying with a partner really helped. We would go through questions, discuss the psychology behind them, break down why one answer was stronger than another, and talk through moments where we doubted ourselves. That added a layer that solo review often misses.

Prepsaret helped reinforce the information I was getting from Rita's and Study Hall, and it pushed my thinking closer to PMI's framework in a more active way.

David McLachlan (YouTube)

Free, and worth the time.

What stood out to me about David McLachlan's content was the way he explained the reasoning behind the answer choices. A textbook can give you the rule. He often helped clarify the why behind it.

When something was not clicking through reading alone, his videos often helped it land faster. During my final stretch, I watched one of his full PMP walkthrough videos and took notes the entire time. I cross-referenced those notes with Rita's, Study Hall, and Prepsaret to reinforce the areas where I was still getting things wrong.

If you learn well by hearing concepts explained and walked through, do not overlook that resource.

PMBOK Guide (8th Edition)

I would not treat the 8th Edition as a replacement for the foundation you already built. Think of it more as a supplement, especially for candidates testing closer to the July 2026 exam refresh and beyond.

It is helpful for understanding areas such as value delivery, tailoring, accountability, quality, sustainability, and the seven performance domains. It also reflects the direction PMI is moving, including discussion around newer project considerations such as AI.

Used the right way, it adds context. It should not replace your core process of study, correction, and review.

Agile Practice Guide

If agile or hybrid questions keep costing you points, this guide deserves serious attention.

For me, it was helpful because it pushed beyond definitions and into behavior. It helped clarify how agile principles actually show up in execution, delivery, governance, and decision-making. That matters, because many candidates understand agile in theory but still miss agile and hybrid questions when those principles appear inside real scenarios.

Pay close attention to life cycle selection, servant leadership in practice, backlog-based delivery, feedback loops, and tailoring. This guide helps connect PMI principles to agile behavior without losing sight of the governance PMI still expects you to respect.

How These Tools Worked Together

One mistake I made early was treating my study resources as interchangeable. I would move between them based on mood instead of purpose. That was part of the noise.

These tools helped most when each one had a defined role.

PMI membership and PMI's guides were my source of truth. Study Hall was my diagnostic tool. Rita's was my process map and reinforcement tool. Prepsaret was my pressure test and discussion tool. David McLachlan was a strong reset point when the text was not landing. The PMBOK 8th Edition and Agile Practice Guide served as useful supplements, especially as the exam continues to evolve.

Used that way, they stopped being random resources and became one connected system.

And the thread tying them all together was my Book of Wrongs. That is what helped turn information into correction, correction into alignment, and alignment into instinct.

APPENDIX C

The 49 Processes: A Mindset Snapshot

One of the steps in building the Book of Wrongs was writing out the 49 processes, not as a memorization exercise, but as a sequence-awareness exercise.

For the exam structure I prepared under before July 2026, "first," "next," and "most appropriate" questions showed up often enough that sequence awareness mattered. Knowing where a process lived in the project flow, what came before it, what came after it, and what it allowed you to do, helped me answer those questions without guessing, especially in predictive and process-driven scenarios.

The descriptions below are written in my own words, not copied from any PMI publication. They are not official definitions. They are short prompts designed to help you understand what each process is really doing and why it matters.

Your job is to read this list, then rewrite it in your own notebook or document.

Handwriting these processes, or writing them from memory and using this list as a check, was one of the most effective ways I built sequence awareness for the version of the exam I took. It helped me stop seeing the processes as isolated terms and start seeing them as a flow.

This is not a table. It is a list. The visual map is yours to build.

Integration Management

- Develop Project Charter — officially starts the project and gives the project manager authority to lead it, once approved.

- Develop Project Management Plan — pulls all subsidiary plans and baselines into one coordinated plan the team can execute against.

- Direct and Manage Project Work — carries out the planned work, coordinates execution, and produces the project's deliverables.

- Manage Project Knowledge — uses existing knowledge and captures new lessons learned so the team can make better decisions as the project moves forward.

- Monitor and Control Project Work — checks overall performance against the plan and identifies where action is needed.

- Perform Integrated Change Control — reviews change requests across the whole project and decides whether to approve, reject, or defer them.

- Close Project or Phase — formally finishes the project or phase, confirms completion, closes records, and releases resources.

Scope Management

- Plan Scope Management — defines how scope will be planned, defined, validated, and controlled.

- Collect Requirements — gathers and documents stakeholder needs so the project knows what it must deliver.

- Define Scope — turns requirements into a clear description of the project boundaries and deliverables.

- Create WBS — breaks deliverables into manageable work packages that can be assigned, tracked, and controlled.

- Validate Scope — gets formal acceptance of completed deliverables from the customer or stakeholder.

- Control Scope — monitors scope and manages changes so the project does not drift into uncontrolled expansion.

Schedule Management

- Plan Schedule Management — defines how the schedule will be developed, maintained, and controlled.

- Define Activities — identifies the actual work actions needed to produce the deliverables.

- Sequence Activities — puts the work in logical order by identifying dependencies and the right flow of activities.

- Estimate Activity Durations — determines how long each activity is likely to take using available data, assumptions, and expert judgment.

- Develop Schedule — builds the full project schedule by combining activities, durations, dependencies, and constraints.

- Control Schedule — monitors schedule performance and manages changes to keep the project on track.

Cost Management

- Plan Cost Management — defines how costs will be estimated, budgeted, and controlled.

- Estimate Costs — develops an approximation of the financial resources needed for project work.

- Determine Budget — aggregates estimated costs to establish an approved cost baseline.

- Control Costs — tracks spending against the budget and manages cost changes.

Quality Management

- Plan Quality Management — defines quality standards and how they will be achieved and measured.

- Manage Quality — ensures quality is built into the process through continuous improvement and correct practices.

- Control Quality — inspects deliverables to verify they meet defined quality standards.

Resource Management

- Plan Resource Management — defines how team and physical resources will be acquired, managed, and used.

- Estimate Activity Resources — determines what resources are needed for each activity.

- Acquire Resources — obtains the team members and physical resources required for the project.

- Develop Team — improves team capability, cohesion, and performance.

- Manage Team — tracks team performance, provides feedback, and resolves issues.

- Control Resources — ensures physical resources are available and used effectively.

Communications Management

- Plan Communications Management — defines how information will be shared, when, and with whom.

- Manage Communications — ensures project information is created and distributed effectively.

- Monitor Communications — verifies communication needs are being met and adjusts as needed.

Risk Management

- Plan Risk Management — defines how risk management activities will be conducted.

- Identify Risks — identifies potential risks that could affect the project.

- Perform Qualitative Risk Analysis — prioritizes risks based on probability and impact.

- Perform Quantitative Risk Analysis — analyzes the numerical effect of risks on project objectives.

- Plan Risk Responses — develops strategies to address threats and opportunities.

- Implement Risk Responses — carries out planned risk response actions.

- Monitor Risks — tracks identified risks, identifies new ones, and evaluates response effectiveness.

Procurement Management

- Plan Procurement Management — defines what needs to be purchased and how it will be acquired.

- Conduct Procurements — selects sellers and awards contracts.

- Control Procurements — manages relationships, performance, and contract changes.

Stakeholder Management

- Identify Stakeholders — identifies stakeholders and analyzes their interests and influence.

- Plan Stakeholder Engagement — defines how stakeholders will be engaged throughout the project.

- Manage Stakeholder Engagement — communicates and works with stakeholders to meet their needs and expectations.

- Monitor Stakeholder Engagement — tracks stakeholder relationships and adjusts engagement strategies as needed.

APPENDIX D

PMBOK 8 Cheat Sheet: Language, Lens, and Your PM Instinct

A standalone reference for candidates testing near or after the July 2026 PMP exam update.

What PMBOK 8 Actually Changes

PMBOK® Guide — Eighth Edition keeps the principles-and-performance-domains foundation of the Seventh Edition while simplifying the principles into six core principles, retaining seven performance domains, and reintroducing process guidance through five project management Focus Areas: Initiating, Planning, Executing, Monitoring and Controlling, and Closing.

PMI also highlights expanded coverage of AI, PMOs, and procurement, with continued emphasis on value delivery, adaptability, accountability, and real-world application.

For PMP candidates, the biggest change is not that you need a completely new study system. The bigger shift is that PMI is signaling more scenario language around value, outcomes, stakeholder context, sustainability, accountability, and adaptive judgment.

PMI's July 2026 exam update also explicitly adds topics such as AI, sustainability, and stakeholder engagement while putting more weight on outcomes and value.

You do not need a separate PMBOK 8 study plan. You need to recognize the new language and map it to the PM Instincts you have already built through this book.

PMBOK 8 Concept Cheat Sheet

For each concept: the key idea, what PMI is often rewarding, which instinct it maps to, what exam language may sound like, and what not to overreact to.

Holistic View

Key idea: See the full system — stakeholders, environment, interdependencies, and long-term consequences — before acting.

PMI often rewards: The PM who reads the broader context before deciding, not just the visible issue in front of them.

Instinct: #1 — Analyze Before You Act

Exam language may sound like: "considering the broader organizational impact," "accounting for long-term effects," "stakeholder ecosystem."

Do not overreact to: This does not mean always delaying action. It means widening your context window before you move. PMI lists "adopt a holistic view" as one of the six core principles.

Focus on Value

Key idea: Decisions are anchored in benefits, outcomes, and strategic alignment — not just scope delivery.

PMI often rewards: The PM who connects work to value throughout the project, not only at the end.

Instinct: #1 and #4

Exam language may sound like: "business case alignment," "benefits realization," "value delivery," "outcomes versus outputs."

Do not overreact to: This does not mean interrogating every micro-decision against strategy language. It means keeping value visible throughout execution, not burying it in initiation and closure.

Embed Quality

Key idea: Quality is built into the way the work is designed, managed, and delivered — not inspected in at the end.

PMI often rewards: Prevention first, then verification.

Instinct: #3 — Protect Compliance and Quality

Exam language may sound like: "quality built into the process," "proactive quality management," "prevent issues early."

Do not overreact to: Inspection still matters. Prevention is usually the stronger first move, but a sound quality system still includes review, validation, and control.

Accountable Leadership

Key idea: The PM leads with responsibility, clarity, ethics, and judgment.

PMI often rewards: Decisive, transparent leadership that respects governance and team ownership.

Instinct: #2 — Coach or Facilitate Before Escalating

Exam language may sound like: "the PM is responsible for...," "ethical obligation," "organizational accountability," "transparent communication."

Do not overreact to: This does not mean the PM makes all decisions unilaterally. Servant leadership and accountability are not opposites.

Sustainability

Key idea: Project decisions carry environmental, social, and economic consequences beyond the immediate deliverable.

PMI often rewards: Long-term impact awareness alongside short-term delivery.

Instinct: #4 — Recognize the Methodology

Exam language may sound like: "environmental impact," "long-term consequences," "social responsibility," "sustainable outcomes."

Do not overreact to: Sustainability is a lens, not a veto. The PM considers it, but does not stop the project over it without analysis.

Empowered Culture

Key idea: Teams that are engaged, psychologically safe, and self-managing deliver better outcomes.

PMI often rewards: Servant leadership that actively builds team capability and removes barriers, not passive noninterference.

Instinct: #2 — Coach or Facilitate Before Escalating

Exam language may sound like: "psychological safety," "team empowerment," "removing impediments," "collaborative environment."

Do not overreact to: Empowered culture does not mean no structure. Self-managing teams still need coaching, clear boundaries, and a PM who removes blockers.

AI / Digital Implications

Key idea: AI and digital tools affect how projects are planned, monitored, and delivered. The PM needs to account for new risks, stakeholder dynamics, and governance considerations.

PMI often rewards: Thoughtful adoption — neither blind enthusiasm nor reflexive avoidance.

Instinct: #4 — Recognize the Methodology

Exam language may sound like: "AI tool introduced to the project," "data privacy concerns," "automated reporting," "stakeholder concerns about automation."

Do not overreact to: You do not need deep technical AI expertise. Apply standard PM logic: assess impacts, engage stakeholders, manage risk, follow governance, and align to value.

PMI says PMBOK 8 expands AI coverage, and the 2026 PMP update adds AI-related topics to the exam.

Exam Weighting — July 2026 Forward

PMI has published rebalanced domain weights for the revised PMP exam launching globally on July 9, 2026:

- People: 42% → 33%
- Process: 50% → 41%
- Business Environment: 8% → 26%

What This Means for Candidates

People still matters, but it is no longer carrying the same relative exam weight as before. Leadership, conflict, motivation, coaching, and servant leadership remain important. Instinct #2 lives here.

Process remains a major scoring area, covering planning, execution, monitoring, and control across predictive, agile, and hybrid contexts. Instincts #1, #3, #4, and #5 still matter heavily here.

Business Environment becomes significantly more important. Strategy alignment, stakeholder value, benefits, compliance, sustainability, and other organization-level considerations deserve more deliberate attention in your study plan. This is where much of the newer PMBOK 8 language is likely to feel most visible.

ECO Exam Structure — Confirmed July 9, 2026

- Exam time: 230 minutes → 240 minutes (10 extra minutes)

- Breaks: One 10-minute break → two 10-minute breaks
- Predictive / agile split: 50/50 → 40% predictive, 60% agile + hybrid
- Total questions: 180 (175 scored previously → 170 scored + 10 unscored pretest)

Source: PMI PMP Examination Content Outline, July 2026

How to Use This Appendix

Read each concept once. For each one, write which PM Instinct it maps to in your Book of Wrongs.

When a scenario uses PMBOK 8 vocabulary, map it to the instinct rather than to a definition. Your response logic should stay the same even when PMI changes the framing.

Use this appendix as a vocabulary bridge, not a separate system. The PM Mindset, PM Alignment, and PM Instinct framework you built through this book still applies. The language is newer. The thinking is the same.

When you miss a question involving sustainability, value delivery, empowered teams, or AI language, tag it here and note which instinct it maps to. That tag becomes part of your Book of Wrongs and keeps your corrections organized around one system instead of scattered across multiple frameworks.

PMBOK 8 is a language and lens upgrade. Your PM Instinct is still the engine.

APPENDIX E

30-Day Study Plan for the Plateaued or Post-Fail Candidate

How to Use This Appendix Alongside Your Existing Materials

This plan is designed for the candidate who has already studied — has Rita, has Study Hall, knows the material — but keeps scoring in the 65–73% range or has already failed at least once. This is not a start-from-scratch plan. It is a correction plan.

WEEK 1 — DIAGNOSE BEFORE YOU ACT (Days 1–7)

This week mirrors Instinct #1. Before touching new content, understand what the score report is actually telling you.

Day 1: Read your score report carefully. If you do not have one, take one full mock exam today (Prepsaret or PMI Study Hall). That result is your score report for this plan.

Day 2: Map your weakest domain to specific task areas using PMI Study Hall's task-level performance data. Write down your 3–5 weakest task statements by name. Do not guess. Look at the data.

Day 3: Read Chapters 1–3 of this book. Do not take notes. Just read. Connect the story to your experience.

Day 4 — PM Mindset vs. PM Instinct (Deep Dive): Read Chapter 4 — The Mindset, the Alignment, and the Instinct carefully.

Rebuild the PM Mindset vs. PM Instinct comparison table in your own words. Capture what changes when mindset becomes instinct.

Highlight the signs that you have the PM Mindset and the signs that you are starting to develop the PM Instinct.

Optional: Use Appendix A as a quick reference once your own table is complete, but do not skip the exercise of writing it yourself.

Day 5: Read the 5 PM Instincts Decision Filter page. For each instinct, write one sentence about how you typically violate it in practice.

Day 6: Set up your Book of Wrongs using the templates in Chapter 7. Do not log entries yet. Just build the structure.

Day 7: Rest. Review what you mapped. Make sure your top 3 weakest task areas are written clearly and visible.

WEEK 2 — TARGETED CONTENT REPAIR (Days 8–14)

This week is precision surgery on your specific weak areas. No broad studying.

Days 8–9: Go into PMI Study Hall and complete the lessons for your weakest task area from Day 2. Read carefully. Extract key insights into your Book of Wrongs.

Days 10–11: Repeat for your second weakest task area. Cross-reference with the relevant chapter in Rita's PMP Exam Prep and the corresponding section in PMBOK 7 — principles, not ITTOs.

Day 12: If an agile or hybrid scenario type is among your weak areas, spend this day in the Agile Practice Guide — specifically life cycle selection, servant leadership, backlog delivery, and feedback loops. Log any new insights.

Day 13: Run 20 targeted questions in your weakest task area, using Study Hall or Prepsaret. Log every wrong answer in your Book of Wrongs.

Day 14: Review all Book of Wrongs entries logged this week. Which instinct appears most often? That is your primary correction target.

WEEK 3 — ACTIVE PATTERN BUILDING (Days 15–21)

The goal shifts from content absorption to pattern recognition.

Days 15–17: Resume broader question practice — 30–40 questions per day across all domains. Log every wrong answer. Prioritize the Book of Wrongs review over the score.

Day 18: Review all current Book of Wrongs entries. Write one correction rule per pattern cluster. These should be in your own words.

Day 19: Take one full mock exam, 180 questions, timed. Do not focus on the score. Focus on whether your documented patterns are still appearing and whether you caught them in real time.

Day 20: Spend three hours reviewing the mock exam miss by miss. Update your Book of Wrongs. Add any new instinct violations.

Day 21: Watch David McLachlan's YouTube series on any concept that is still not clicking. No new question banks this day.

WEEK 4 — CONSOLIDATION AND TRUST (Days 22–30)

The final phase belongs to consolidation, not new content. You are building the reflex, not the toolkit.

Days 22–24: Read your full Book of Wrongs every day. No new questions. Only pattern review and rule reinforcement.

Day 25: Write your top 5 personal wrong-answer patterns on one page. Under each pattern, write the instinct it violates and the correction rule that prevents it.

Days 26–27: Run 50-question timed sets on alternating days. After each set, review misses against your top 5 patterns. Are the same patterns still appearing? If yes, restate the rule. If no, that pattern has moved to instinct.

Day 28: Rest day. Sleep, exercise, and step away entirely. Fatigue erases instinct. Preserving your energy in this final stretch is a performance strategy, not weakness.

Day 29: Final Book of Wrongs review. Read Appendix A. Visualize the exam: scenario appears, instinct fires, right answer arrives.

Day 30: You are ready. Trust the work.

A Note on Integrating Your Other Resources

Rita's PMP Exam Prep: Use it as a process-flow reference, not a reread. Rewrite the Process Chart from memory. If a task area is weak, read the corresponding Rita chapter once, then run questions on it.

PMI Study Hall: Your primary diagnostic tool and the closest simulation to the real exam. Use the task-level data to track whether gaps are actually closing. Do not use it mindlessly — every session should have a target task.

Prepsaret: Timed pressure simulation. Use it for stress-testing your reasoning in the final two weeks. Fifty-question timed sets are more useful than full-length simulations at this stage.

PMBOK 7: Read for principles, not memorization. If a People or Business Environment scenario does not make sense, the answer is almost always in one of the 12 principles. Read the principle. Then reread the scenario.

Your Book of Wrongs is the thread that connects all of them. If Rita explains something you missed, log the insight. If Study Hall reveals a pattern, log the entry. Every resource feeds the Book of Wrongs. The Book of Wrongs builds the instinct.

APPENDIX F

PM Instinct Master Sheet

A Write-It-3-Days-Before-the-Exam Operating System Built from PMBOK 7, Agile Practice Guide, and the PM Instinct Framework from PMP Journey

1. THE DECISION ENGINE

Before you touch the answer choices, run this sequence:

- Locate the scenario — Predictive, agile, or hybrid?
- Initiating, Planning, Executing, Monitoring and Controlling, or Closing?
- Name the real problem — People? Scope? Schedule? Cost? Quality? Risk? Change? Stakeholder? Procurement?
- Use the PM Response Order — your decision spine: Assess → Engage → Review → Process → Document → Escalate

  (Understand root cause first → right stakeholders → plan, charter, risk register → change control, risk response, quality → update artifacts and communicate → only when authority or risk truly requires it)

Auto-eliminate answers that:

- Act before understanding
- Escalate before trying resolution
- Implement unapproved changes
- Ignore stakeholders
- Protect schedule over value, quality, or governance

2. THE 5 PM INSTINCTS

Use these as your built-in filters. For each instinct: first move, wrong move, and what PMI is protecting.

#1 — Analyze Before You Act

Pause first: read the scenario, find root cause, check the plan, talk to people if needed.

First move: Identify what is actually happening before deciding anything.

Wrong move: Any action answer that skips assessment. "Immediately update the schedule" without first analyzing impact.

PMI is protecting: The project from decisions made without full information.

Exam bait: "A risk occurred... a stakeholder is upset... performance dropped..." → do not jump straight to action.

#2 — Coach or Facilitate Before Escalating

Default to servant leadership: coach, facilitate, remove impediments, engage stakeholders.

First move: Coach, facilitate, or engage directly.

Wrong move: Escalate to the sponsor or senior management before trying direct resolution.

PMI is protecting: Team trust, sustainable performance, and the PM's role as a leader — not just a coordinator.

Exam bait: "Team conflict... low morale... resistant stakeholder..." → do not jump to authority or escalation.

#3 — Protect Compliance and Quality

Prevention before inspection: standards, training, early testing, proactive risk responses.

First move: Investigate root cause and implement corrective action.

Wrong move: "Monitor and document" when a proactive option is available.

PMI is protecting: Cost of quality. Prevention is always cheaper than post-defect correction.

Exam bait: "Audit finding... process deviation... no defect yet..." → fix the process now.

#4 — Recognize the Methodology

Read the world: contract type, life cycle, governance, team maturity, stakeholder ecosystem.

First move: Identify the environment — predictive, agile, or hybrid — and the governance layer, then apply the appropriate behavior.

Wrong move: Apply a generic rule regardless of context. Mix agile and predictive behaviors in the wrong environment.

PMI is protecting: Sound judgment. PMI rewards the PM who reads the room.

Exam bait: "Sponsor requests a feature... CCB mentioned... sprint mentioned..." → know which world you are in.

#5 — **Trust Your Trained First Answer**

After you apply the instincts, your first answer is usually right. Changing answers without new information breaks alignment.

First move: Check: do I have new information, or is this anxiety?

Wrong move: Changing your answer because two options "both seem possible."

PMI is protecting: Nothing. This instinct protects you from yourself.

3. PM RESPONSE ORDER — THE EXAM DECISION SPINE

When two answers both sound good, ask: which one follows the proper PM Response Order?

1. Assess — Understand the issue before acting. Review the scenario, identify root cause, confirm the methodology, and identify the domain or process area involved.

2. Engage — Speak with the team member, stakeholder, product owner, sponsor, vendor, or customer as appropriate. Clarify first. Facilitate first. Coach first.

3. Review — Check the plan, charter, risk register, communications plan, quality management plan, backlog, contract, stakeholder engagement plan, or other relevant artifact.

4. Process — Apply the correct PM action: change control, risk response, quality management, issue resolution, stakeholder engagement, backlog reprioritization, retrospective follow-through, or escalation if warranted.

5. Document — Update artifacts and communicate outcomes.

6. Escalate — Last resort only, after 1–5 are exhausted or blocked.

Any answer that jumps to #6 without evidence of 1–5 is almost always a trap. Any answer that skips #1 and acts immediately is almost always wrong.

4. CONTEXT QUICK RULES

Predictive environment: If baselines move, formal change control. The size of the change is irrelevant. If a Change Control Board exists, nothing gets informally approved. For schedule compression, analyze crashing versus fast-tracking before acting, then submit a change request if the baseline is affected.

Agile environment: The team owns the work. The product owner owns the value. The PM facilitates. Sprint commitment is a team agreement, so protect it. Stakeholder engagement is continuous, not milestone-gated. Change is built in, but it still goes through the team's process.

Hybrid environment: Honor the governance requirements of the predictive portions. Honor self-organization in the agile portions. Do not mix behaviors across boundaries.

5. ELIMINATION RULES

These answer patterns are almost always wrong:

- Escalate immediately without trying direct resolution
- Approve a change informally
- Act before assessing or analyzing the situation
- Reassign a struggling team member without coaching first
- Document stakeholder disengagement without investigating it
- Apply predictive change control to a clearly agile scenario
- Apply agile flexibility to a clearly predictive scenario
- Report status without data or forecast

6. DOMAIN REMINDERS

People domain: Coach before reassigning. Facilitate before escalating. Engage before documenting. Stakeholder disengagement is a risk, not paperwork.

Process domain: Change control applies to all baseline-affecting changes regardless of size. Quality management means designing for quality first, then verifying. Risk management means responding per plan and reassessing residual risk afterward.

Business Environment domain: Benefits realization is ongoing, not post-delivery. Governance obligations supersede team comfort. Compliance issues must be reported through proper channels, not handled privately.

"This is not a substitute for the Book of Wrongs. It is a product of it. Build yours from your own patterns — then you will own every line."

Acknowledgments

To the individuals who provided me with the resources and connections to get into the PMP bootcamp when I faced obstacles — your generosity moved the journey forward when it could have stopped.

To my friends and family members who offered encouragement throughout — your belief carried more weight than you may ever know.

To my study buddies and accountability partners along the way — iron sharpens iron, and you sharpened me.

To all of you, I have much gratitude. Thank you.

About the Author

Cartraill Love is an author and PMP-certified project leader whose journey reflects the power of resilience, disciplined thinking, and personal transformation.

After failing the PMP exam twice, he refused to walk away. Instead, he studied his mistakes, reworked his thinking, and built a system that turned frustration into clarity and correction into progress. That process ultimately led to Above Target performance across all three domains and inspired the frameworks at the heart of this book, including the Book of Wrongs and the 5 PM Instincts.

His work is grounded in a simple belief: growth is found not only in success, but in the courage to confront failure, learn from it, and keep moving forward.

Through WAGA Solutions and a growing body of work spanning professional development, creative enterprise, and personal transformation, Cartraill continues to build systems and frameworks aimed at helping people think differently, perform better, and move forward with purpose.

Call to Action

If this book helped you think differently about the PMP journey, keep going.

Visit mattersofmatterspublishing.com/pmpjourney for additional resources, tools, and support to help you strengthen your PM Mindset, PM Alignment, and PM Instinct.

www.ingramcontent.com/pod-product-compliance
Lightning Source LLC
Chambersburg PA
CBHW072101150726

47999CB00005B/1824